MEMORIALS TO THE ROMAN DEAD

MEMORIALS

SUSAN WALKER

TO THE ROMAN DEAD

Published for the
Trustees of the British Museum by
British Museum Publications Limited

© 1985 The Trustees of the British Museum

Published by British Museum Publications
46 Bloomsbury Street, London WC1B 3QQ

British Library Cataloguing in Publication Data

Walker, Susan
  Memorials to the Roman dead.
  1. Funeral rites and ceremonies–Rome
  I. Title
  393'.0937   GT3252.A2

  ISBN 0–7141–1275–5

Designed by Harry Green

Typeset and printed in Great Britain by the Pindar Group of Companies,
Scarborough, North Yorkshire.

Contents

Acknowledgements

I should like to thank John Wilkes, Brian Cook and Lucilla Burn for reading and commenting on drafts of this text, an expanded version of a public lecture given at the British Museum in February 1984, following the opening of four of the Wolfson Galleries of Classical Sculpture and Inscriptions. My thanks to Bill Cole, and to Ivor Kerslake and Tony Cowell of the British Museum photographic service.

The information on the quarries at Proconnesus is derived from a paper by Dr Nuşin Asgari, published in the *Proceedings of the Xth International Congress of Classical Archaeology, Ankara 1973* (1978). The translation of Polybius' account of events at Roman funerals is adapted from that of E. S. Shuckburgh (1889). The evidence for cremation rites is based upon research on cremation burials from Ephesus by Dr Theya Molleson and Michael Bowmer.

This book is dedicated to the memory of two great scholars who first aroused my interest in Roman sculpture and the marble trade: Donald Strong and John Ward-Perkins.

SUSAN WALKER
August 1984

Abbreviations

CIL	*Corpus Inscriptionum Latinarum* Berlin, 1863
GR + number	Greek and Roman Antiquities + date of registration in the departmental collections of objects not included in published catalogues.
GIBM	*The Collection of Ancient Greek Inscriptions in the British Museum* (1874–1916; reprinted in facsimile edition Milan 1979)
Sc + number	A. H. Smith, *A Catalogue of Sculpture in the Department of Greek and Roman Antiquities, British Museum* Vols. I–III (1896–1904).

Introduction: a Roman funeral

In the summer of AD 14 the first Roman emperor, Augustus, died while residing at an estate belonging to his family at Nola, near Naples. The magistrates of the intervening *municipia* (established communities on which Roman status had been conferred) and *coloniae* (settlements founded and populated by Rome) were charged with the responsibility of carrying the emperor's body to Bovillae, a small town near Rome which had some association with the imperial family. There it was placed in the care of Roman knights, members of a class that had been highly favoured during Augustus' reign. They brought the body into Rome and placed it in the entrance-hall of the emperor's residence on the Palatine Hill. All these journeys were made by night. In the hot daylight hours the corpse reposed in the basilicas (halls of justice) of the towns whose magistrates were charged with its care.

Augustus' funeral procession was headed by a statue of Victory which normally stood in the senate-house. The spectators did not see his body, but an image of him made of wax and dressed as if to celebrate a military triumph. The body was hidden from view in a funerary couch of gold and ivory, draped with gold and purple hangings. Two images of the deceased emperor accompanied the cortège: one of gold had been brought from the senate-house, and another was drawn in a triumphal chariot. Behind these were other images intended to set Augustus in his place in Roman history. These included portraits of his ancestors and relatives (though not his adoptive father Julius Caesar, who after his assassination in 44 BC had been declared a god), and of distinguished Romans, both legendary and historical, from Romulus, the founder of Rome, to the general Pompey the Great, the defeated enemy of Julius Caesar.

Two orations were given when the procession reached the Forum. Augustus' stepson Tiberius, who ten years previously had been reluctantly adopted by the emperor as his heir, spoke in front of the temple of the deified Julius Caesar; another eulogy was delivered by Tiberius' son Drusus in front of the *vetera rostra*, the platform traditionally used for orations in the Forum, which was decorated with the prows of captured ships and statues of distinguished Romans. Senators then carried the body to the Campus Martius (Field of Mars) by the Tiber, where it was placed upon a pyre. The priests, followed by cavalry and infantrymen, circled round it. Any who possessed triumphal awards threw them on the pyre, which was set alight by centurions. An eagle was released and flew to heaven, foreshadowing the flight of the emperor's spirit. His widow Livia, whose name had been changed by his will to Julia Augusta, stayed five days by the pyre. The most prominent knights then collected Augustus' bones. Barefoot and bereft of any insignia of their rank, they placed the bones in the huge mausoleum Augustus had ordered to be built in the Campus Martius at the outset of his career as ruler of Rome in 31–28 BC (1).

The need to assert political supremacy at Rome had provided the rationale for building this mausoleum. Boldest of all was the future emperor's choice of site: the Campus Martius lay by the bank of the Tiber. Burial here was permitted only by special consent of the Senate and Roman people. Fearing pollution, not only from disease but also in

1. The Mausoleum of Augustus. (Fototeca Unione, at the American Academy in Rome. F.U. 4371 F)

a more spiritual sense, the Romans buried their dead outside the walls of their cities. But Augustus' tomb was linked with a new development of public buildings in the surrounding area.

Augustus and a few other powerful individuals were able to ignore popular revulsion at the presence of the corpse and perpetuate the memory of powerful families by constructing great tombs in the centres of cities. For the first Roman emperor a mausoleum was not enough. Augustus composed the *res gestae*, his own account of his achievements, and had the great bronze plaques nailed to the walls of his tomb. The visitor wandering in the pleasant park surrounding the mausoleum was thus not only confronted by the huge bulk of the tomb, surmounted by a statue of the late emperor, but also by a written account of Augustus' achievements. Throughout Roman history writing played a central part in transmitting the memory of the dead to the living. A permanent record of his or her life was the most an individual could expect by way of a significant memorial.

Ritual at death

If still living, the mother of a dying person was considered most suited formally to end the life of her child. Giving the last kiss she might hope to catch the spirit as it passed from the body with the final breath. She would then close her child's eyes. Afterwards close relatives called out aloud the name of the dead person and began the formal lament. The body was set on the ground, washed and anointed. A Roman man would be traditionally dressed in a toga, coloured according to his rank (p. 11). He might also be crowned with a wreath, especially if he had won a crown for military or civil service in the course of his life. A coin

2. Relief from Amiternum: the funerary procession of a notable. (Museo Archeologico di L'Aquila; photo: I.N. 30.516)

was often placed in the mouth to pay Charon, who ferried the departed across the rivers of the underworld. Distinguished persons might be laid upon a special bed (*lectus funebris*) for as much as seven days while others came to pay their last respects. The poor could expect to be burned or buried the day after their death.

Funerary processions were traditionally held at night. A marble relief from Amiternum (central Italy) portrays the funerary procession of an important person (2). He is shown reclining on a *lectus funebris*, which is set on a bier carried by eight men. A canopy with moon and stars evokes the hour of the procession. Musicians playing horns and pipes lead the way. Male mourners, probably related to the dead man, turn to observe the bier while weeping and beating their breasts. The bier is followed by the women of the family, who cling to each other with gestures of grief. The smaller figures behind them may be professional women mourners hired for the occasion.

The body of Augustus, the first emperor, was burned in the traditional Roman manner. When the emperor Nero's wife Poppaea died in AD 65 she was embalmed, and the historian Tacitus saw fit to remark that she was not burned according to the Roman custom (*Romanus mos*), but was inhumed and embalmed according to the practice of foreign kings. Indeed, for many centuries cremation had been the favoured method of burial at Rome. However, the dictator Sulla (d. 78 BC) was the first member of the Cornelii family to be cremated, and the tomb of the Scipios, located beside the Via Appia near Rome, was found to be filled with inscribed stone sarcophagi (coffins used for inhumations) of the third and second century BC. But these families were exceptional, and cremation was regarded as the norm until a revolution in burial customs took place in the second century AD.

Ritual did not end at burial. Ceremonies carried out on the anniversaries of a death ensured the continued remembrance of the departed amongst relatives, descendants, dependants and friends. Tombs were specially opened for the purpose of sharing meals with the dead. Some evidently believed that the spirits of the departed resided in the ground, at or near the tomb. Food and drink were offered to them through the necks of *amphorae*, pottery storage jars used for burial of the poor (3).

3. Offerings to the dead, made through the necks of *amphorae* (storage jars). (Drawing by Susan Bird)

10

Pipes were cut in the covers of graves for the same purpose; holes cut in the lids of cinerary chests could also accommodate perfumes and liquid refreshment. With regular offerings of flowers and incense the departed were thus always comforted, and the dead, physically separated from the living, were formally reunited with their families and dependants.

Perhaps the most striking aspect of Roman rituals at death is the emphasis placed upon the long-term continuity of the family. To this end images of distinguished ancestors were paraded at the funerals of notable men: these perhaps provided some compensation for the lack of a permanent memorial within the city.

Tacitus records that at the funeral of Augustus' stepson Drusus in 9 BC such images, probably terracotta busts, were placed around the dead man's bier. But the most vivid account of the peculiarly Roman use of ancestral masks was written long before the emergence of an imperial family by the Greek historian Polybius, comfortably exiled to republican Rome in the second century BC.

'Whenever one of their distinguished men dies . . . the body . . . is carried into the forum to the Rostra . . . and sometimes is propped upright upon it to be conspicuous. Then with all the people standing round, his son . . . or . . . one of his relations mounts the Rostra and delivers a speech

4. Inscribed funerary relief with ancestral portraits in cupboards. (Nationalmuseet, Kobenhavn, Antiksamlingen 1187)

on the virtues of the deceased, and the successful exploits performed by him in his lifetime. The people are thus reminded of what has been done, and made to see it with their own eyes – and their sympathies are so moved, that the loss appears public, affecting the whole people. After the burial and all the usual ceremonies have been completed, they place an image of the deceased in the most conspicuous spot in the house, surmounted by a wooden canopy or shrine [4]. This consists of a mask made to represent the deceased both in shape and colour. These images are displayed at public sacrifices and, when any distinguished member of the family dies, they carry these masks to the funeral, putting them on men thought as like the originals as possible in height and other personal peculiarities. These actors dress according to the rank of the person represented: if he was a *consul* [chief magistrate] or *praetor* [judge], a toga with purple stripes, if a *censor* [magistrate in charge of the census of citizens], all purple, if he had also celebrated a [military] triumph, a toga embroidered with gold. The actors also ride in chariots, while the *fasces* [rods] and the axes, and all the other usual insignia of office, lead the way, according to the dignity of the rank in the state enjoyed by the deceased in his lifetime, and on arriving at the Rostra they all take their seats on ivory chairs in their order. There could not be a more inspiring spectacle for a young man of noble ambitions and virtuous aspirations. For can we believe that anyone could not be moved at the sight of all the likenesses of the men who have earned glory, all as it were living and breathing?'

Polybius claimed that the extraordinary rites offered to Roman aristocrats encouraged the younger members of the families to suppress self-interest and win glory in serving the state. Their funeral parades had another effect less publicised by writers biased in favour of the aristocracy. The status of well-to-do families, forbidden the chance to build a tomb in the city, was considerably enhanced by genealogical pageants. Moreover, funeral parades were condoned by many as a morally just and appropriate rite. But other forms of expenditure, for example on elaborately decorated biers, musicians (2), games or banquets, were considered vulgar. Marcus Aemilius Lepidus, chosen leader of the Roman senate six times over a period of twenty-four years, claimed 'the funerals of great men are properly enhanced not by expenditure but by the parade of ancestral masks'. He therefore instructed his sons to carry him to his grave on a bier lined with linen 'without purple'. Expenditure on his own funeral was limited to one million asses. It has recently been calculated that, at the time of this man's death in 152 BC, this sum would have supported up to eight hundred peasant families at subsistence level for a year.

The texts of funerary orations were preserved by great families, much as they collected ancestral masks. Thus it was possible to relate an individual's career and deeds to those of his or her ancestors. Cicero, writing in the last years of the Republic, makes it clear that some families were not above creating a fictitious past, contrived to flatter the family's contemporary status. Unfortunately, few original texts have survived. The most substantial of these, the *Laudatio Turiae*, celebrates the virtues of a noblewoman who died in the reign of Augustus. In it her husband recounts her adventures as a young woman during the civil wars that followed Caesar's murder in 44 BC. The text of the oration was engraved on stone; it appears that the couple intended a permanent record to be inscribed, like the deeds of the emperor, on the walls of the family tomb.

When Mark Antony delivered the oration for Julius Caesar, he interrupted his account of Caesar's deeds with periods of lament and weeping. His audience joined in, as if they were the chorus in a play. Another formal eulogy of Caesar, which may have been given by the *praefica* (a woman who led the lament), included an account of his fate: a representation of Caesar was then made to name his assassins, while a wax model of the murdered Dictator rotated to display his twenty-three wounds. Much of this was political theatre, devised for the occasion to exploit the feelings aroused by Caesar's murder. But many of the elements of the orations were traditional features of Roman funerals. The review of events in life was interwoven with mourning and lament for death. The Romans were not sure of survival after death, and the dead played no central role within organised religious belief. Permanent memorials were crucial to their hopes for immortality, serving a function of little relevance to Christian believers.

So important was the record that many wrote on their tombs that the memorial had been commissioned while they were 'alive and of sound mind'. The desire for a permanent record eventually spread to a wide range of social groups: thousands of Roman imperial tombstones have survived, intact or reused. Many are inscribed. With the descriptions given in the surviving literature, and with the information recovered from excavated burial grounds, the stones of memory give a detailed picture of funeral rites, of the trades associated with burial, and (though the Romans wrote of their dead, as we do, in clichés), of the lives and times of those they commemorate.

Roman cemeteries and tombs

In 1868 the British architect and engineer John Turtle Wood excavated one of the gates of the wealthy city of Ephesus, the major port of the Roman province of Asia. He found two roads leading out of it. That leading south to the city of Magnesia wound, he recorded, 'amongst the substructures of monuments, some of which are of large proportions and very massive and are evidently raised over persons of distinction. These are to be traced for more than two miles beyond the gates'. The other road, to Ayasoluk, the modern Selçuk, was to lead Wood to his goal, the lost Temple of Artemis, one of the Seven Wonders of the ancient world. The road was lined 'with tombs of every description, but chiefly sarcophagi of white marble ... On the side of the mountain near this road an upper road for foot passengers had been constructed with arched recesses where they were required by the irregularities of the natural formation. Many of these recesses had been used as *columbaria*' (literally, dove-cots: chamber-tombs with niches for cinerary chests and urns).

In the course of his search for the lost temple Wood had discovered the Roman and early Byzantine city of Ephesus, and two of the city's major cemeteries. Of these the cemetery by the road to Magnesia seems to have been reserved for Roman and native dignitaries and officials, while the other was used by the humbler classes. Wood was sponsored by the Trustees of the British Museum, and he brought to London examples of memorials from both cemeteries. Among those from the road to Magnesia were two monuments, most probably the tombstones of high-ranking Roman officials, both of whom apparently died while serving as assistant (*legatus*) to the *proconsul* (the Roman governor) of the province of Asia. Carved in relief were the *fasces* (bundles of rods) symbolising their judicial authority; these may have been carried at the head of their funeral processions (p. 12).

The *fasces* flanking the monument to Marcus Helvius Geminus (*CIL* III 6074) were cut from the sides and shipped separately to London.

The inscription records a career touching on many aspects of Roman society. The son of Lucius, of the Falernian tribe at Rome, Marcus Helvius Geminus served as *tresvir auro argento aere flando feriundo* (abbreviated in the text to IIIVIR.A.A.A.F.F.), one of a board of three responsible for the Mint of Rome). He was a member of the Palatine order of Salian priests, a body of free men whose duty it was to observe the opening and closure of the military campaign season with rites, including dances, dedicated to Mars, the god of war. He served on the Rhine as military tribune of the 16th Legion Germanica, disbanded by Vespasian in AD 70, and was then appointed *quaestor* to the emperor (a junior magistrate with the special distinction of liaising between the emperor and the Senate). He was subsequently *praetor* (one of a board of judges at Rome), moving thereafter to the eastern provinces, where he was assistant to the governor of Macedonia, subsequently serving the governor of Asia in the same capacity. The Emperor Claudius, probably in AD 47/8, raised him to patrician rank. He died some time after AD 54, that is after the death of Claudius, who is described in the monument as *divus* (deified).

5. The front of the memorial to Marcus Calpurnius Rufus. From Ephesus. *CIL* III 6072.

Marcus Calpurnius Rufus, son of Marcus, a member of the Collina tribe at Rome, served as prefect in charge of the corn supply at Rome, a post to which he had been appointed by senatorial decree (5). With the rank of *praetor*, he served as assistant to the proconsular governors of Cyprus, Pontus and Bithynia, and Asia. Another source records a man of this name as governor of Achaea (southern Greece) under Hadrian, who sent him an imperial ruling on a point of law: he may be descended from the man commemorated at Ephesus.

A tombstone from Rome records the death at the age of thirty of Titus Aurelius Saturninus, *eques singularis* (a member of the mounted imperial body-guard. Like many of his colleagues, he was born in Pannonia (now Hungary), and served eleven years in the Roman army before dying at Rome. His memorial was set up by his friends and heirs, the standard-bearer Titus Flavius Marcellinus and Titus Aurelius Secundinus. The text and the portrayal below it of a man leading a horse reflect the dead man's career at Rome (6), but the marble of the tombstone is Greek, from Proconnesus, and the representation of the banquet above the text is typical of Greek funerary sculpture. The name

6. The tombstone of the *eques singularis* Titus Aurelius Saturninus. From Rome. *CIL* VI 3222.

Aurelius signifies citizenship granted in the later second or third century AD, by the emperors Marcus Aurelius (AD 161–180) or Caracalla (AD 211–217).

Texts such as these, setting out often with some illustrations the personal lives and careers of Roman soldiers and officials, constitute a unique record of individuals and institutions of the Roman Empire. Much of interest to the social and legal historian may also be learned from Roman wills, which were sometimes recorded in permanent form. One of the most remarkable of these concerns the dying wishes of Sextus Julius Aquila of Andemantunnum (Langres, France). The original text has perished, but was found of sufficient interest to be copied in medieval times (*CIL* XIII 5708). Towards the end of his life Sextus Julius Aquila commissioned a memorial shrine, surrounded by extensive grounds and a lake. In the shrine was to be built an alcove containing a seated statue of the dead man, at least five feet high, made of 'the finest marble from overseas or else of the finest bronze'. Below the alcove was to be set a sedan-chair flanked by two seats, all made of the finest imported marble. Here were to be kept covers, to be spread out on the days when the shrine was opened, and two rugs, two dining cushions of equal size, two cloaks and a tunic. In front of this monument was to be set an altar, carved to the highest standards from the best Luna marble. In this Aquila's bones were to be laid to rest. A slab of Luna marble was commissioned to close the tomb 'in such a way that it may easily be opened and closed again'. A sum of money was provided for the maintenance and repair of the monument and the grounds. Reserve teams of gardeners were appointed in case of need. No one was to be buried nearby, ever. Huge fines were payable to the city in case of violation of the site. On anniversaries the dead man's kinsmen and dependants were to feast at the tomb, remaining there until everything had been consumed. Freedmen were put in charge of maintenance of the site but the arrangements for the great man's funeral were entrusted to his grandson. All his personal effects were to be cremated with him. These included his hunting-gear (nets, spears, a sword, traps and snares are specified), his sedan-chair, his rushboat, and all the medicines he used for study.

Another text, probably from Aquae Sextiae (Aix-en-Provence), is written in Greek in the style of Homeric epic. The text is inscribed in the central panel of the sarcophagus of Proclus, a victor in oratorical competitions (7). His widow Rufina speaks: would that we knew whether she herself had composed the Greek verse.

> You, Proclus, husband of me, Rufina, lie here, by the will of the fates abandoning your life and your widow. I built a great tomb in a prominent site, a wonder to all. I added to it gleaming doors. I put in it a statue closely resembling you, dressed to reflect your distinction among the Ausonian [Italian] orators. Among these illustrious men you took the highest distinction. But never shall I lie apart from you. Just as before in our lifetime the same house protected us, so shall the same sarcophagus enclose our corpses.

This was composed early in the fourth century AD. During Proclus' lifetime the Roman world had witnessed protracted civil wars and the rise to power of emperors of humble provincial background and mili-

7 Part of the sarcophagus of Proclus.
From Aix-en-Provence (?). Sc.2314.

tary training. Diocletian, the most remarkable of these, had directed a complete reorganisation of imperial administration. At the time of Proclus' death Christianity was on the point of becoming the official religion of the Roman state. None of this is evident from the surviving parts of his coffin, which reflect the traditional interest taken in Greek culture by the Provençal intelligentsia. Proclus is portrayed to the left of the inscribed panel, dressed as a Greek orator and resting upon a column. The branches beside him reflect his success in oratorical contests. This scene, and the sentiments expressed in his epitaph, would have been understood two centuries and more before his death, for Proclus' memorial evokes the world of the second century AD, when the philhellene Emperor Hadrian raised the Greek provinces of the empire from a state of comparative neglect to one of high fashion. It was indeed the vogue for Greek culture spread by Hadrian, who personally visited every province of the Roman Empire, which led to the adoption by Romans of Greek sarcophagi for burial, in place of the traditional Roman practice of cremation, the cremated bones being kept in urns or altars such as that specified by Julius Aquila. By the third century the use of sarcophagi had spread almost to the outer limits of the empire: fragments of a Greek marble sarcophagus have recently been excavated as far afield as Welwyn, in Hertfordshire.

Another inscribed plaque, like that commissioned by Rufina for

17

Proclus, reflects the wishes of a woman, Aurelia Felicissima, responsible for ordering the family tomb (*GIMB* 1026). This text, like the will of Sextus Julius Aquila, includes prohibitions on the use of the tomb by unauthorised persons. The name of the woman, which is misspelled in the text, indicates that she was of humble birth. The specific mention of Proconnesian marble as the stone used to make the most elaborate sarcophagus in the tomb may reflect the spread in the third century AD of sculptured marble sarcophagi to people of humble origin, who were proud to precisely record for posterity their choice of burial chest.

> Aurelia Filikistima bought this tomb and the platform and had made for it a sculptured sarcophagus of Proconnesian marble and sarcophagi on each side and a millstone (sarcophagus). She prepared the burial chamber for herself and her husband Epiktetos, for their children and their descendants. No-one has the right to burial here unless they are of the family. If anyone dares to bury here anyone who is not a kinsman or a member of the family, he shall pay to the *aerarium* [i.e. the Treasury, the Latin word is transliterated into Greek] of the Roman people 2,500 denarii. A sealed copy of this inscription was deposited in the record office five days before the kalends of June, the fourth day of the month of Hekatonbeion [28 May; Hekatonbeion is a month of a Greek calendar used at Smyrna].

Sarcophagi and the marble trade

The will of Sextus Julius Aquila (p. 16) bears witness to the high regard in which Luna marble was held. Greatly exploited for cinerary urns and altars, the quarries at Luna (Carrara, Tuscany) were not a significant centre for the production of sarcophagi. This is probably because sarcophagi were in origin a Greek fashion, and, when demand for them spread through the Roman Empire, the Greek quarries came to dominate the market. Nonetheless, a considerable number of lids of Luna marble were produced (9). These were made to fit the bodies of sarcophagi sent to Italy roughly cut from the Greek quarries to be decorated in Rome. Many must have arrived without lids, and some may have suffered damage in the voyage. There were, moreover, customers requiring a personalised inscription; this would most likely be carved on a lid of Luna marble.

Most quarries producing cinerary chests and urns catered for a limited local market. Some of these survived into the era of large sarcophagi: the quarries at Belevi, serving the city of Ephesus and the Cayster valley, are one of many examples of such a survival. The characteristic form of Ephesian sarcophagi, which had gabled lids and bodies decorated with garlands suspended from the skulls of sacrificial beasts, was very similar to that of the much smaller *osteothekai* (chests for cremated bones) made at the same quarries in the first century AD (pp 55-7;fig.10). Sarcophagi made of Belevi marble were hardly exported outside the region; a few are known from the Maeander Valley to the south, but exports further afield are rare. The long-distance trade was dominated by three quarries (8): Mount Pentelicus (in Attica, north-east of Athens), Proconnesus (now the island of Marmara in the sea of the same name) and Docimeum (near the modern town of Karavaç in west central Turkey).

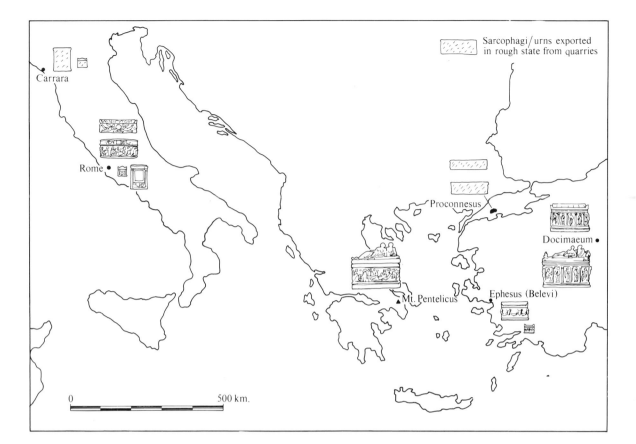

Sarcophagi/urns exported in rough state from quarries

Carrara

Rome

Proconnesus

Docimaeum

Mt. Pentelicus

Ephesus (Belevi)

0   500 km.

8. Map showing the major marble quarries producing sarcophagi. (Drawn by Susan Bird)

9. Part of a lid of a sarcophagus, made of Carrara marble: cupids at play. GR 1947.7–14.5.

10. The cinerary chest of Pannychus, Pithane and Pithane. From Ephesus. Sc.1275.

11. Part of an Attic sarcophagus found at Xanthos, south-west Turkey. Sc.957a + b.

Mount Pentelicus

The quarries north-east of Athens produce a fine-grained marble famous for its luminosity. This was the marble used to build and decorate the Parthenon. It may be crisply and delicately carved with a chisel, and weathers to an agreeably warm honey tone. Pentelic marble contains much iron, and veins of mica run at random but frequent intervals along the bedding lines. It is difficult to cut large blocks of Pentelic marble without encountering such faults. Another difficulty is caused by the location of the quarries, which entailed considerable haulage overland to reach Athens and the port of Piraeus.

Pentelic marble is not mentioned in the Edict on Maximum Prices issued by the Emperor Diocletian in AD 301. By that time it is likely that the quarries were no longer significantly exploited. The recommended price for this marble in Roman times thus remains unknown. The characteristics mentioned above probably made it relatively expensive. Certainly Attic sarcophagi were very grand in scale (11), and were normally decorated on all four sides, which suggests that they were intended to be displayed beside a road, perhaps within the walls of a family graveyard.

12. A sarcophagus from Crete, made to imitate the Attic style of decoration. Sc.2324.

In the second century AD Attic sarcophagi, like those made at Belevi and elsewhere in Asia Minor, were commonly decorated with garlands suspended from the skulls of sacrificial animals (12. This is an imitation made in Crete of local stone). Attic sculptors were also fond of *erotes* (cupids: the children of Venus), and portrayed them carrying garlands in the centres of the fronts of sarcophagi. Entire sarcophagi might be decorated with engaging scenes of *erotes* at play. Paired griffins set on either side of a candelabrum were also a popular form of decoration (11). Early Attic sarcophagi were covered by gabled lids. The figured scenes were framed above and below by elaborately decorated mouldings.

In the third century AD mythological scenes became popular. Many were drawn from a very conservative repertoire of themes, some of which had appeared in the decoration of the Parthenon, such as battles between Greeks and Amazons and scenes from the Trojan wars. The scenes were often framed at the sides by caryatids, architectural supports derived from representations of the women of Caryae, a city in the Peloponnese enslaved by the Greeks for having sided with the Persians in the wars of the early fifth century BC. On Roman sarcophagi the caryatids stood on moulded plinths decorated with figures of animals associated with hunting (13).

The universally popular earlier form of decoration with garlands gave sarcophagi the appearance of miniature shrines. This may have reflected the status of all containers of human remains, which were sacred in the eyes of Roman law (p. 58). There may also have been some intention of suggesting that the dead were to be regarded as heroes, a notion implied in later figured sacophagi, in which a dead man might be equated with a hero such as Achilles or Meleager.

13. An Attic sarcophagus from the same site as 12: scenes from the life of Achilles. Sc.2296.

The lids of later Attic sarcophagi were often made in the form of ornately upholstered beds (14). On these were set reclining figures, evidently intended as portraits of those (usually a man and woman) who had commissioned the sarcophagus. The bodies were finished in the workshops associated with the quarries, but the heads were left roughly carved to be completed by a local workshop on the arrival of the sarcophagus at its destination. Illustrated here is the lid of an Attic sarcophagus found at Cyrene (Libya) where the bed and the torsoes of the figures are finished but the heads are contoured only with a point (15). Such heads were commonly left unfinished, possibly for lack of skilled craftsmen at centres far from the quarries, or because the sarcophagus was urgently required. Finished heads from an Attic sarcophagus found at Sidon (Lebanon) still have stone supports for the backs of the necks of the reclining figures (16; also Sc.2012).

The practice of portraying the dead lying on a funerary couch was probably derived from monuments popular in the first century AD, especially at Rome, in which marble or terracotta effigies appeared reclining on beds set on low platforms, which were often decorated in

Sc 2367 **Rome**

Sc 2418 **Rome**

Sc 2350 **Rome**

Sc 2323 **Rome**

GR 1947.7-14.8 **Rome**

Sc 1274 **Ephesus**

Sc 1282 **Ephesus**

Sc 2296
Attic. Crete

Sc 2301 **Phrygian. Athens?**

Phrygian.
Antalya Museum

0   2 m.

24

14. Some typical forms of sarcophagi and
cinerary urns. Reconstructed lids of
sarcophagi in the British Museum
collections are shaded. (Drawn by
Susan Bird)

15. Unfinished portraits on the lid of an Attic
sarcophagus exported to Cyrene, Libya.
(Photo V.M. Strocka)

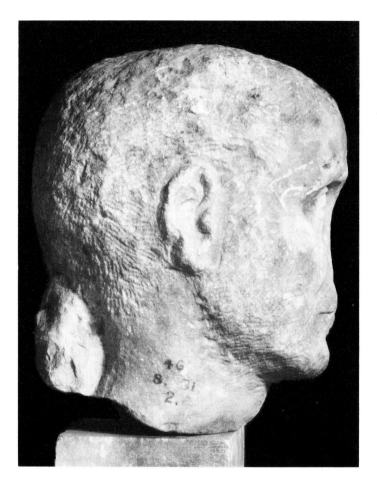

16. Finished head from the lid of an Attic sarcophagus exported to Sidon, Lebanon. Sc.1955.

relief. None of these has been found serving as the lid of a sarcophagus; indeed, the reclining figures later passed out of fashion at Rome. On one monument (17), a reclining woman holds a portrait bust of a man, probably her husband who died before her. Their hairstyles evoke the fashions of the court of the Emperor Trajan (AD 98–117). The monument is made of costly Parian marble, not greatly exploited for sarcophagi but much favoured for portrait heads, as the stone could be highly polished to give a convincing impression of refined white flesh, unused to exposure to the sun through outdoor labour.

The Etruscans, too, had favoured burial chests decorated with Greek myths and with reclining figures, also apparently portraits of the deceased, upon the lids (18). Most of these were designed to hold cremated bones. They were made locally of native limestones and alabasters. Very popular in the second century BC, when much of Italy came under strong artistic influence from Hellenistic Greece, these were gradually abandoned in favour of the more severe memorials typical of later republican Rome. Many families must have survived into the imperial era, and it is unlikely that Etruscan family vaults, many of which contained large numbers of these chests, would have been forgotten.

26

17. Woman reclining with a
portrait bust of a man.
Probably from Rome. Sc.2335.

18. Etruscan cinerary urn with
young man reclining on the lid.
On the body, the death of
Eteocles and Polynices.
From Chiusi. D. 40–41.

Proconnesus

Proconnesus is the ancient name of the largest of a group of islands in the Propontis (the Sea of Marmara) between the Bosporus and the Dardanelles. The northern part of the island is entirely made of marble, mostly rather coarse-grained (in comparison with Luna or Pentelic) and not luminous. The marble is greyish-white, with striking parallel bands of blue or grey. Though it may seem to many a less attractive stone than Pentelic, marble from Proconnesus has two advantages over its Attic counterpart. Most varieties of Proconnesian marble contain little mica, and are not prone to faults which cause the stone to splinter. Proconnesian marble may thus be quarried in large blocks, and, as the quarries are near the sea, these may be loaded onto boats with the minimum of transport overland. Quarrymen are still working on Proconnesus, producing blocks used for veneer and fittings in bathrooms. These are roughly worked in small workshops near the quar-

19. Unfinished Proconnesian sarcophagus exported to Odessus (Varna, Bulgaria). (Photo by Susan Walker)

ries, to be polished on arrival at the point of resale (which may be as distant as Syria). This practice saves weight in transporting and adds to the value of the product before resale.

Modern activity in the quarries has provided an opportunity for rescue excavations and the installation of an open-air museum at the port of Saraylar. The excavations have revealed that the quarries operated in antiquity much as they do today, but on a considerably larger scale. The excavators found a cemetery of faulty sarcophagi, in each of which several skeletons were interred, apparently the members of families of quarrymen. An inscription on one such sarcophagus, like that set up by Aurelia Felicissima threatened would-be violators with a fine, in this case payable to the harbour-master and the 'friends of Cyzicus', the nearest mainland city in whose territory the island lay.

The excavators also found many artefacts only roughly cut, including architectural elements (such as column capitals and bases), sarcophagi and statues; some are of considerable scale. The archaeological evidence from Saraylar points overwhelmingly to activity in the Roman imperial period. It seem likely that the Proconnesian quarries were imperially owned, but no evidence has survived for their administration in the early empire. Proconnesian marble is listed in the Edict issued in AD 301 by the Emperor Diocletian; the recommended price is relatively low.

Other indications have survived of Proconnesus' renown throughout classical antiquity. Vitruvius, a native of Italy who wrote a treatise on architecture during the reign of Augustus, records that this was the source of one of the prized marbles selected for the decoration of the tomb of Mausolus at Halicarnassus (south-west Asia Minor), built in the middle of the fourth century BC and regarded as one of the Seven Wonders of the ancient world. One of the earliest exports from Proconnesus is an inscribed stele 2.30m high found at Sigeum in the Troad. This, one of the Elgin Marbles now in the collections of the British Museum, was erected about 550 BC to commemorate the gift to the council of Sigeum of a wine-bowl, a strainer and a stand by Phanodicus of Proconnesus (*GIBM* 1002). Vitruvius says that Proconnesian marble was shipped to Ephesus for use in the Temple of Artemis, built in the second half of the sixth century BC, though this assertion remains archaeologically unproven.

This perhaps more than any other marble was used in antiquity for sculpture, sarcophagi, architectural elements and for cladding walls and paving floors. Sarcophagi made here for the local market, for the Black Sea, the Danube regions, and for the Levant were, like Attic sarcophagi, of formidable scale, with steeply pitched and gabled lids (19). Decoration of the body was often restricted to inset panels carved with figured scenes, frequently adapted from the decoration of earlier tombstones. *Tabulae ansatae* (literally, panels with handles) were also made, inscribed with appropriate texts. The Proconnesian workshops also produced large numbers of the sarcophagi decorated with garlands familiar to other ateliers.

In the third century AD it appears that large numbers of Proconnesian sarcophagi were exported to Rome, the largest market in the

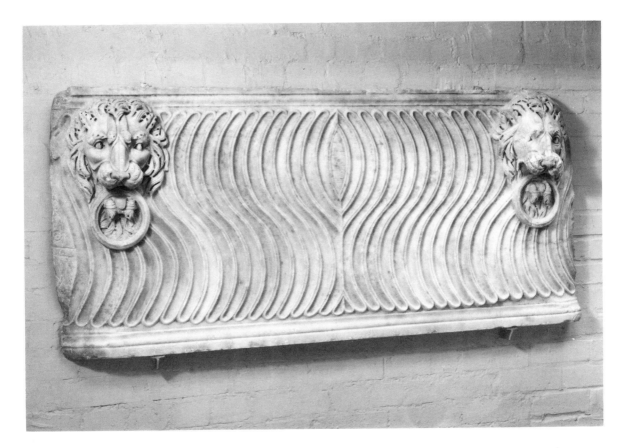

20. The front of a Proconnesian marble *lenos* decorated with lions' heads. Probably from Rome. GR 1914.6–27.3.

empire. These were sent roughly cut from the quarries, and at Rome they were decorated with scenes quite alien to the traditions of the workshops on Proconnesus. Many were shaped at the quarries to resemble the *lenos*, a vat used for treading grapes. A shipwreck of *lenoi* was discovered off the south coast of Italy at San Pietro near Taranto some twenty years ago. The meagre evidence for dating the wreck suggests that it occurred in the third century AD. The earliest *lenoi* were appropriately decorated at Rome with scenes from the life of the wine-god Bacchus. A more formal scheme of decoration was later evolved, in which the front of the *lenos* was covered with channels cut to resemble the strigil used to scrape oil from the body at the gymnasium. The front of the sarcophagus was further ornamented with two projecting heads of lions, at first shown snarling (Sc.2338–9) and later with ring-shaped handles clamped between their jaws (20). In the San Pietro wreck the lions' heads appear as roughly shaped rectangular bosses. Some later versions of *lenoi*, mostly made in the second half of the third century AD, were decorated with full figures of lions creeping around the curved sides of the sarcophagus to pounce upon their prey. Usually accompanied by a trainer, these are thought to represent circus lions. Analysis of stone from several examples of the earlier types of *lenos* suggests that they were made of Proconnesian marble. *Lenoi* decorated with circus lions were apparently made of a greater variety of marbles. It is possible that supplies to Rome from the quarries around the

Aegean Sea were temporarily disrupted by the barbarian invasions of Greece and western Asia Minor in AD 267-8.

Many of the lions' manes are the work of virtuoso sculptors, with deeply drilled channels emphasised by decorative bridges of marble. That they were regarded as distinctive in antiquity is suggested by the plaque commemorating the Greek-speaking Christian sculptor Eutropus, buried in a cemetery by the Via Labicana, Rome (21). The sculptor is shown at work on a lion's mane, aided by an assistant who rotates the drill-strap. This may be Eutropus' son, who dedicated the plaque. Though Eutropus apparently specialised in sarcophagi decorated with lions' heads, his memorial shows that his own inscribed sarcophagus was decorated with dolphins. These may refer to his journey to Rome if, as seems possible, he was a first-generation immigrant.

A huge variety of sarcophagi was produced at Rome, many apparently of Proconnesian marble. A characteristic shape, especially of some later models, is a rectangular box much lower than those made in Greece and Asia Minor (14). The relatively modest scale may reflect the cost of transporting the roughly worked stone. The repertoire of mythological and other decorative themes was enormous, reflecting the size and social range of the local market. Many sarcophagi were carved at Rome for export to the western provinces.

As Proconnesian marble was more easily obtainable than Pentelic or marble from Docimeum, it was sometimes used to make imitations of other types of sarcophagus. Part of a sarcophagus found near Sparta, in southern Greece, is decorated with scenes of a battle between Greeks and Amazons (22). The theme, the style of the moulded frame above (only partially finished) are characteristic features of Attic sarcophagi.

21. Inscribed and decorated *loculus*, a memorial to the sculptor Eutropus. From the Via Labicana, Rome. (Museo Civico, Urbino: photo: I.N. 75.1102)

22. Part of a Proconnesian marble sarcophagus found at Sparta, made to imitate the Attic style of decoration. Sc.2304.

The marble has been scientifically analysed and appears to be Proconnesian; it could have been sent to Sparta by sea and river. A number of similar sarcophagi are known from Sparta: they may have been inspired by the import of a genuine Attic sarcophagus. The form of this group of sarcophagi suggests that, even though they were not made of Pentelic marble, the Attic style was preferred. It is unusual to find a Proconnesian marble sarcophagus in southern Greece, where the Attic workshops were dominant. Indeed, there is relatively little overlap between the markets of sarcophagi made in the three major quarries. Their workshops tended to serve markets located in areas of traditional interest to the cities in whose territory the quarries lay. Thus Pentelic sarcophagi were exported in large numbers throughout Greece and Crete, and to Cyrenaica in North Africa and to the northern countries of the Levant, while Proconnesian sarcophagi were sent to Alexandria, to ports on the coast of the Black Sea and on both sides of the Adriatic. Though all major producers are represented at Rome, it was marble from Proconnesus that dominated the metropolitan market.

Docimeum

'Beyond is the village of Dokimia, and the quarry of Synnadic stone (for that is what the Romans call it; the locals call it Docimite or

Docimaean). At first only small blocks were extracted from the quarry, but on account of the extravagant taste of the Romans for columns they now cut huge monoliths resembling alabaster in the diversity of their colours. Though the transport by sea of such heavy cargoes is difficult, both columns and veneer are conveyed to Rome, a source of wonder for their size and beauty' (Strabo, *Geography*, XII, 8,14).

Written in the age of Augustus, this account reveals the extent of Roman appreciation of Phrygian marble. The quarries produce a violet and white marble known as pavonazetto (this is the alabaster-like stone noted by Strabo) which lies embedded in a fine-grained translucent white marble. From at least the middle of the first century AD the quarries were imperially owned, and were administered by officials known as procurators, drawn from the ranks of former slaves of the imperial family. The recommended price for Docimaean marble in late antiquity, given in the Edict of Diocletian, was relatively high.

It has recently been established that, in the second and third centuries AD, Docimeum was the main centre of production of the sarcophagi decorated with figures set between projecting columns

23. Child's sarcophagus of Phrygian marble. From Crowe's Tomb, near Benghazi, Libya. Sc.2326.

which have long been recognised as originating from Asia Minor. The Phrygian quarries were far from the sea. To judge from their findspots, the sarcophagi were sent by road throughout Asia Minor and by the rivers Hermus and Maeander to the west coast. Some were shipped to Italy, Greece and the Levant. Like other ateliers of the Greek east, the Phrygian workshops also produced sarcophagi decorated with garlands supported by *erotes*. The example illustrated (23) was made for a child and comes from a chamber-tomb near Benghazi, Libya. But sarcophagi decorated with figures set between columns were the most characteristic products of the workshops at Docimeum. Some of the motifs were derived from gravestones which had long been popular in Phrygia: doors set in an ornate architectural frame were especially popular and were adapted to decorate the short sides of columnar sarcophagi. The earliest of these are elegant, with restrained architectural decoration. The front of a sarcophagus illustrated here (24) shows

24. The front of a Phrygian sarcophagus decorated with the labours of Hercules. Said to be from Athens. Sc.2301.

34

scenes from the life of Hercules, a motif which may have suggested personal qualities of industry and persistence in the face of adversity. A similar example now in the museum at Antalya (southern Turkey), most likely the product of the same workshop, has its gabled lid preserved.

The notion of placing figures in a sequence between columns to tell a story may be traced to the funerary art of the fourth century BC. The 'Mourning Women' sarcophagus from Sidon, now in Istanbul Museum, has such a scheme of decoration. Free-standing figures (some are displayed in the British Museum in rooms 12 and 81) were set between the columns on the podium of the tomb of Mausolus, dynast of Caria (south-west Asia Minor) who died in 353 BC. Some are thought to represent Mausolus' ancestors and members of his court.

In the third century AD Phrygian sarcophagi followed contemporary trends and became much more ornate, with more direct references to

25. Figure, possibly a portrait, from a Phrygian sarcophagus. GR1947.7–14.12j.

the person or persons who had commissioned them. A considerable depth of stone was now cut out behind the columns and the figures, throwing them into high relief. The entablatures above the columns were intricately decorated with patterned mouldings. Though the rendering of the drapery was rather summarily achieved with chisels, use of the vertically held and running drill in the hair and in architectural decoration was exuberant and effective (25). Indeed, it may be claimed that Phrygian sculptors were the first to create the lacy effect which was later to become a distinctive feature of Byzantine architectural decoration.

The earlier type of Phrygian columnar sarcophagus was about 2.5m long and over 2m high. The later models, like those made in Attica, had lids with figures reclining upon beds: these might be nearly 4m long and well over 3m in height (14). As in the case of Attic sarcophagi, the size and ornate decoration of Phrygian sarcophagi must have reflected the status and wealth of their owners. Their form may have intentionally copied the decoration of contemporary public buildings. Often given to the community by Roman officials or by local notables, these were decorated with marble figures, which frequently included portraits of the donor and members of his or her family, members of the imperial family, historical or legendary founders of the city, and personifications of the donor's virtues. Like the figures on Phrygian sarcophagi, these were packed into niches framed by projecting columns, which both enhanced the sculptures and protected them from the weather. Indeed, the growth of the trade in Phrygian marble sarcophagi coincided with a remarkable increase in the construction of such public buildings in the cities of Asia Minor. By the third century AD even small communities in areas remote from the major roads and rivers boasted buildings decorated with marble.

The representation of individuals

Within a century of Hadrian's death (AD 138) the trade in marble sarcophagi had spread to all provinces bordering the Mediterranean Sea and to many inland areas accessible by river or road. As the demand grew, so did a taste for the representation of individuals who were to be buried in the sarcophagus. The taste for portraits was nowhere more apparent than at Rome, where individuals often appeared in the centre of the front of their sarcophagus. They might commission a straightforward portrait, set in a medallion (26) or in a shell, or even appear as the hero or heroine of a myth (27). The sleeping Endymion or Ariadne were obvious choices for the portrayal of the dead, but the range was wide and, to modern eyes, puzzling. Some women chose to appear as the lovelorn suicides Stheneboia and Phaedra, while a man might be portrayed as Admetus, the unfortunate husband of Alcestis who found snakes in his bridal chamber. This practice stood in striking contrast to the portrayal of individuals on sarcophagi made for markets in the Greek east. On Attic sarcophagi portraits were apparently confined to figures on the lid. Similar portraits were made for the lids of Phrygian sarcophagi, but some of these also included figures set between columns which may have been intended as portraits or as heroised representations of the dead (25). At many quarries in Asia Minor conventionally decorated sarcophagi were given a personal touch by setting portrait busts above the garlands. This was done as early as the middle of the second century AD.

At Rome interest in portraying the dead as gods or heroes had gained ground before sarcophagi were greatly used in the first century AD. Under Claudius (AD 41–54), the practice of representing the emperor and members of his family as gods had become widespread, and the distinction between the living emperor and his deified ancestors had become blurred. In the course of Claudius' reign many former slaves of the imperial family held high office and exercised considerable power in affairs of court and state. The fashion for representing the dead as

26. Portrait of a man set in a medallion, from the front of a Proconnesian marble sarcophagus made at Rome. Sc.2323.

27. Young man portrayed as the sleeping Endymion, on the front of a Proconnesian marble *lenos* made at Rome. GR1947.7–14.8.

28. Relief from the tomb of a woman, portrayed here as Victorious Venus. GR1948.4–23.1.

gods spread from the families of these men to other well-to-do slaves and freedmen. It was considered especially appropriate for women, children and youths, but a businessman might also choose to reflect his success by having himself represented as his patron god Mercury. By the end of the first century AD, after sixteen years of rule by Domitian, another emperor who permitted freedmen of his family to hold high office, many appeared as gods in their tombs, which had come to resemble temples decorated with galleries of statues. Such symbolism was an innovation, with no clear precedents in later Greek or Italic funerary art: it may well have been regarded as vulgar and 'arriviste' by long-established Roman families.

One relief from a tomb (28) portrays an unnamed woman as the goddess Victorious Venus. By the sixteenth century the tomb it adorned had been destroyed, and the relief was reused, along with three others from the tomb, in a fountain in the garden of a villa in the centre of Rome. Two of the other reliefs are now lost, but some idea of the tomb may be retrieved from a drawing of the reliefs in the fountain made in the sixteenth century. The woman's hairstyle indicates that the tomb was built during the reign of the Emperor Hadrian (AD 117–138). A second panel similar to that in the British Museum apparently portrays the same woman as a priestess. A third decorated with figures of the Three Graces may have been intended to illustrate the woman's personal qualities of grace and charm; a fourth, now built into a wall in Richmond, Surrey, shows a bust evidently representing the same woman borne aloft by two cupids.

The form of the tomb as a shrine to the qualities of the dead is well illustrated by the recently reconstructed façade of the Library of Celsus at Ephesus (29). Tiberius Julius Celsus Polemaeanus served the Emperor Domitian (AD 81–96) as Minister of Public Building and Works. He was subsequently appointed governor of the province of Asia, and donated a magnificent library to Ephesus, its most outstanding city. After his death in AD 116 his son Celsus Aquila completed the library as a memorial to Celsus Polemaeanus, who was buried inside it in a

29. Reconstructed façade of the Library of Celsus at Ephesus. (Photo by Susan Walker)

40

marble sarcophagus. On the façade of the building statues personifying Wisdom, Moderation and other virtues were set in niches protected and enhanced by projecting columns. The inscribed bases have survived, making it clear that the statues referred to Celsus Polemaeanus' personal qualities. Flanking the façade, raised on high bases above the courtyard, were bronze statues of Celsus Polemaeanus and the emperor, both portrayed on horseback. The inscribed base of the imperial statue listed the emperor's full titles; that of Celsus Polemaeanus similarly reviewed in detail his military and political career.

Social status is also made clear in the gravestone of Agathemeris, daughter of Aphrodisios of the Attic deme of Kollyteos, and of her husband Sempronios Niketes of the same deme (30). Agathemeris may have commissioned the tombstone while still alive. On it she is portrayed standing beside her husband and dressed in the fringed cloak, knotted between the breasts, that was the privilege of initiates to the cult of the Egyptian goddess Isis. Agathemeris carries the *sistrum* (rattle) and *situla* (pail) used in the rites of the cult. Evidence from

30. Tombstone of Agathemeris and Sempronios Niketes. From Athens. Sc.630.

D · M ·
OCTAVIO ISOCRHY
SO FILIO DVLCISSIM
Q · V · ANN · D · XX ·
CRHYSEROS ET
PRIMITIBA PAREN
ΕΥΥΥΧΙ ΓΛΥΚΟΝ

similar tombstones and from other inscriptions suggests that initiation was a privilege reserved for the daughters of well-to-do Athenians. Agathemeris' husband has a Roman name; the relief probably dates to the second century AD. The faces of husband and wife were both deliberately mutilated, probably by Christians.

In antiquity many people died unexpectedly of diseases now considered curable. Sarcophagi were frequently purchased from stock in haste; portraits roughly cut in the workshop sometimes required drastic alteration. Thus the portrait of the infant Octavius Isochrysus, who died at the age of one year, had clearly been intended by the sculptor as a portrait of a woman, whose head was hastily transformed into that of a male infant with close-cropped hair (31). Even more striking is a figured *lenos* originally intended to show a woman in the role of Ariadne, wife of the wine-god Bacchus. But the sarcophagus was urgently required for a young man, so Ariadne's breasts were cut down and her head turned into a portrait of a youth with a shaven head typical of the militaristic fashion of mid-third-century Rome (27). It is a style that jars with the feminine limbs of Ariadne, still preserved in the lower part of the figure.

Many children were commemorated with scenes evoking happier times. A relief in the Townley collection portrays a boy fishing; it was dedicated by his foster-brother (Sc.648). The sarcophagus of the

32. The sarcophagus of Lucius Aemilius Daphnus: boys playing with nuts. Sc.2321.

plebian boy Aemilius Daphnus, a member of the unprivileged lower orders at Rome (32), is decorated with lively scenes of boys playing with nuts; a dignitary of Ferentinum in central Italy is known to have made provision in his will for a gift of nuts to the children of the plebs, whether slaves or free-born (*CIL* x 5853). The front of another child's sarcophagus is whimsically decorated with cupids mimicking the rites of the wine-god Bacchus (33). Some children's sarcophagi were given a personal meaning, not by a portrait but by an inscription naming the child and his grieving parents. Such an inscription would normally give the exact age of the child at death, in years, months and days. This

33. The front of the sarcophagus of Leontius: cupids mimic the rites of Bacchus. Sc.2316.

information might also be given in a memorial for an adult who had died prematurely. The accompanying dedication was often sentimental in tone:

> To the spirits of the departed and to Lucius Aemilius Daphnus of the Pomptine [voting-tribe]. He lived 4 years and 6 days. Livia Daphne (had this made) for her dearest son.
> (Sc.2321: see fig.32)

> To the departed spirits and to our dearest son Octavius Isochrysus, who lived 1 year and 30 days. His parents Chryserus and F(lavia?) Primitiba [sic] (had this made).
> The Greek inscription simply states 'Farewell, suffering one'.
> (Sc.2322: see fig.31)

> . . . us (his) father to his son Leon(t)ius, most dear beyond all (bounds of) love, who lived 8 years and . . . months.
> (Sc.2316: see fig.33)

Inscriptions might also state the social rank of the parents and even of the child. This is particularly true of later imperial texts, notably of those from tombs located near the imperial frontier. This fashion may have derived from the army, and from a desire to emphasise the distinctions between Roman citizens and the native population.

> To the departed spirits of Sallustius Iasius, son of Gaius. Domitius, treasurer of the Imperial accounts, together with his wife Sallustia Caeliana, had this made for his well-deserving foster-son, who lived 5 years. To the well-deserving one.
> (Sc.2317; from Rome)

> To the spirits of the departed. To Ulpia Aurelia Valeria, a young girl already betrothed [?], 3 years, 9 months, 17 days, daughter of Aurelius Herculanus, His Excellency with the rank of *ducenarius*, who lived for 13 years [sic], 8 months, 16 days. (This was dedicated) to their most dutiful granddaughter by Ulpius Valerius Aurelianus, His Excellency with the rank of *centenarius*, and Titania Mansueta, a woman who wears the *stola*. Traveller, stop and read. Nothing could be found crueller than this monument.
> (Sc.743: see fig.34)

On the latter monument, a limestone slab over two metres high found at the Greek city of Tomis (Constanța, Romania), Ulpia Aurelia Valeria appears in a vignette above the text (34). Though only three years old

35. The tombstone of Avita. Sc.649.

34. Tombstone of Ulpia Aurelia Valeria. From Tomis (Constanța, Romania). Sc.743.

when she died, she is portrayed the same size as the adults who recline on the couch next to her wicker chair. Servants stocking the table beside the couch are diminutive by comparison with the other figures. The message is spelled out in the text. At this period (the late third century AD), *ducenarius* and *centenarius* were honorary titles awarded for civilian and military service to the emperor. The *stola* was a garment worn by women of equestrian rank. The traveller invited to stop and read 'for nothing may be seen crueller than this monument' might be as much impressed by the status of this family as by their fulsome expressions of loss.

On a relief in the Townley collection, wealth and leisure are implied by the image of a young girl, portrayed seated and reading from a scroll with another scroll set on a lectern nearby (35). At her feet a pet dog implores her to forget her learning and go out to play. The inscription beneath reads: 'Avita, having lived 10 years and 2 months. Farewell [passers-by].'

In Augustan Rome it had been the fashion for freedmen to be portrayed with other members of their families (36) on framed reliefs set into the walls of their tombs (Sc.2276, 1954.12–14.1). The figures appeared as if in a window. The portraits were often surrounded by symbols of trade. Beneath were cut simple inscriptions naming those portrayed and sometimes also others who had set up the tomb. Though the people thus commemorated were aliens, as is clear from the accompanying inscriptions, they chose to be portrayed in a traditional Roman style which in the republic had been reserved for members of the

36. Relief of the freedman corn-merchant Lucius Ampudius Philomusus, portrayed with his wife and daughter. From Rome. GR 1920.2–20.1.

37. Relief portrait of . . . bolis son of Iodranos and Atilia Eutychides. Found in the River Thames, this was probably acquired by the Earl of Arundel. Sc.2272.

aristocracy. In effect the style had become a sign of Roman identity. It may have been intended to suggest that the person so portrayed was to be considered morally Roman, that is to be associated with the old-fashioned republican virtues of austerity, severity and respect for old age and for figures of authority, or simply that it was now possible for the families of freedmen to respect their parents and emulate their deeds, just as the sons of Roman aristocrats had done in the Republic.

As a result of Augustan legislation it had become possible for the children of some freedmen to become Roman citizens. Later generations of freedmen at Rome appear to have abandoned memorial portraits of traditional Roman form: instead they had their cremated bones interred in fancifully decorated and inscribed urns and altars. But the republican style of portrait spread to the small towns of Italy and thence, with help from the army and veteran soldiers, to the remoter provinces. At Rome itself the style enjoyed a revival under the Flavian emperors (AD 70–96). Vespasian, the first of the dynasty victorious in the civil wars of AD 69, himself originated from the small Italian municipality of Rieti (Reate), and was no doubt anxious to present to his subjects a changed image from that of the last member of Augustus' family, the decadent Nero (AD 54–68).

Two reliefs both portray couples, shown frontally in the republican style, but with Roman imperial hairstyles suggesting a date of about AD 100 (37; also GR.1919.11–19.1). The reliefs probably derive from the northern shores of the Aegean Sea; one was found by soldiers of the First Leinster Regiment while digging trenches for the front line of the Macedonian campaign of 1916. The inscriptions show that none of the named individuals was a Roman citizen, but the portraits suggest a Roman identity. Many provincials continued to present themselves as Romans long after the citizens of the metropolis had contrived a Greek style of hair and dress.

38. Child's sarcophagus of Proconnesian marble: the marriage of Cupid and Psyche. From Rome. Sc.2320.

Scenes apparently representing marriage have been recognised on a large number of sarcophagi made for the market at Rome. Some of these may reflect missed opportunities. A small sarcophagus in the Townley collection, no doubt intended for a young girl, is decorated with a charming and witty portrayal of the marriage of Cupid and Psyche (38). Musicians accompany the feast; rabbits, a symbol of fertility, play beneath the marriage bed. Similarly the cupids playing with armour on the sarcophagus of Sallustius Iasius may have alluded to a forfeited military career. Rather different in character is a group depicted on a fragment of a large sarcophagus in the Townley collection (39). A man and a woman, the latter veiled, stand with right hands joined (*dextrarum iunctio*). Between them stands another veiled woman, while a youth attends the man, who holds a scroll in his left hand. The pair in the foreground are evidently intended to represent man and wife. Against the wife's skirt lie the remains of a torch, held by a figure of cupid (now missing). The heads and feet of all the figures are restored. Conventionally interpreted as a representation of the rites performed at marriage, it is perhaps more likely that the scene represents an idealised act of worship of personifications of qualities closely associated with marriage: *concordia* (harmony) and *pietas* (dutifulness). Better preserved scenes of this type suggest that they were especially favoured by the equestrian order (Roman knights). An urn in the same collection depicts Vernasia Cyclax and her husband, a freed slave of the Imperial family and 'scribe of the bedchamber', with their right hands joined in a gesture of matrimonial harmony (*CIL* VI 8769). The letters FAP below the scene may describe the deceased woman as faithful, affectionate and dutiful [*f(identissimae), a(mantissimae), p(ietissimae)*].

Some sarcophagi evoked the pathos of premature death. Though these were decorated with genre scenes available from stock, they convey a sense of mourning before burial. On one sarcophagus for a child (40), a personal touch is given by the small sandals beneath the bed, and the dog beside them who plays with a garland fallen from the girl's lifeless hand. Veiled in mourning, mother and father sit at each

39. Part of a sarcophagus of Proconnesian marble representing a married couple and attendants. From Rome. Sc.2307.

40. Child's sarcophagus: lament around the
death-bed of a young girl. From Rome. Sc.2315.

end of the bed making gestures of grief. Hired women mourners, their
hair dishevelled, weep and wail around the bed. A male mourner
stands behind the father's chair, his tunic pulled down to the waist to
beat his breast. Another similarly dressed stands behind the mother. A
woman tears her hair behind the mother's chair, while another repeats
the mother's gesture of mourning. A partially preserved sculpture in
the Townley collection was also intended to convey pathos (Sc.1930).
Carved almost in the round, it represents a sleeping infant wearing
across his chest a band of *crepundia* (amulets). This was probably intended to be set on the child's tomb. The *crepundia* perhaps recalled the
personal insignia by which well-to-do children were identified when
given to the care of a wet-nurse.

Memorials for the cremated

A young girl on her death-bed is apparently the subject of a funerary
relief in the Townley collection (41). She is named on the bed-frame
and in the inscribed panel below as Cornelia Onesime. The text of the
panel explains that she was the household servant of Cornelius
Diadumenus and Cornelia Servanda, and died at the age of nine years,
five months and twenty-eight days. Below the bed a hungry bird
threatens a table laid with a funerary meal. To either side of the bed are
busts, probably intended by Diadumenus to represent her master and
mistress, themselves former slaves. However, the relief was bought
from stock, and the busts had been intended by the sculptor to
represent two men. One of them has been left unfinished; perhaps there

50

was no opportunity to alter it to a portrait of Cornelia Servanda, who died, we are told in the text, at the age of sixty. The reclining figure on the bed also has a masculine appearance; this may be why the bed-frame is labelled with the dead girl's name.

The style of the busts indicates a date in the late first century AD. At this period, however grand their tomb, most Romans, including members of the imperial family, were cremated. The customary Roman practice was to place the cremated bones in urns or chests. These were

41. Relief of Cornelius Diadumenus, Cornelia Servanda and Cornelia Onesime. From Rome. Sc.2363.

42. Cinerary chest of Gaius Magius Heraclides. From Rome. Sc.2370.

of an astonishing variety (14): some were made of alabaster or onyx; many more were of marble, often elaborately decorated. Some took the form of shrines, with side walls cut to resemble ashlar masonry, and with gabled roofs often fitted with miniature tiles and antefixes at the corners. The front of one unusual chest from the Townley collection (42) is divided by columns into four compartments, each marked by a pair of doors with a curtain hanging above. An articulated pediment decorated with animals associated with hunting unites the four sections. The sides of the chest are marked only by a diagonal cross. At the back, however, the side walls are recessed and moulded at top and bottom, and the mouldings are continued around the back of the chest. Only one of the front compartments bears an inscription on the curtain. This commemorates Gaius Magius Heraclides, son of Quintus, enrolled in the Palatina voting-tribe of Rome, who died aged eighteen.

The chest (Sc.2369) containing the ashes of Publius Licinius Successus was fashioned like a shrine with side-walls cut to imitate ashlar masonry. On the front were two cupids holding a garland, a motif popularly used for the decoration of sarcophagi. Above the garland a small cupid rides a sea-panther. Other containers resembled altars; the larger models were treated architecturally. The lids of many chests were perforated to allow the pouring of libations (offerings of wine or oil) to the dead.

Since most chests were set in niches, the finest decoration was reserved for the front, where vignettes might appear of scenes later to be carved in detail upon the fronts of sarcophagi. A cinerary chest dedicated by her husband to the spirits of Junia Pieris has in the centre of the front a portrait of the deceased woman set in an ornate medallion flanked by griffins and by pilasters decorated with vines (43). The woman's hairstyle suggests a date in the early years of the second century AD. The motif was probably copied from much larger reliefs set in tombs, such as a contemporary portrait bust of a man, said to have come from Rome (44). The portraits on Proconnesian sarcophagi made

43. The cremation chest of Marcus Junius Hamillus and his wife Junia Pieris, portrayed in a medallion. Sc.2367.

M·I·VNIVS·M·L
HAMILLVS·SIBI·ET
IVNIAE·PIERIDI
CONIVGI·CARISSIMAE

at Rome in the third century AD (e.g. Sc.2323) no doubt were derived from these. But most decoration of urns and chests was embellishment, in the form of trees, fruit, flowers, animals, birds, and so forth, surrounding a panel inscribed with the name of the dead and that of the person who had set up the tomb. The inscriptions were simpler than those of later Roman memorials. The most outstanding moral qualities of the dead person might be mentioned, and the exact age, especially in cases of premature death. The names of persons subsequently interred might be added to the bottom of the panel.

44. Portrait of a man, set in a wreath. GR 1914.6–24.4.

Evidence for cremation rites

Three chests found by John Wood by the road leading from Ephesus to Selçuk still contain cremated bones (Sc.1274, 1275, 1276). These are of particular interest, since the evidence recovered from the cremated remains may be compared with that offered by the inscriptions on the outside of the chests, which are otherwise conventionally decorated with garlands suspended from the skulls of sacrificial animals. One chest was commissioned for Anassa, daughter of Apollonius, 'a worthy woman'. The Greek inscription contains no other information besides a conventional expression of farewell. The cremated bones found in the chest belonged to two individuals. Both lack male characteristics, and show a remarkable similarity in the degree of burning, which suggests that they were cremated at the same time. It is impossible to identify the women; no age at death is given for Anassa, and no mention is made in the text of a second individual.

Another chest, inscribed in Greek and Latin, was commissioned for Pannychus, for his wife Pithane and for his daughter, also called Pithane (10). Inside were found the cremated remains of two adults, possible Pannychus and his wife. The man, who died in old age, shows little trace of wear on his joints. He was apparently not employed in physical labour; some connection with the Roman administration of Ephesus might be inferred from the bilingual inscription. With the cremated remains were found the unburned bones of a child aged about seven. Their state suggests that they had been interred in the ground before being put in the chest. If they represent the remains of Pannychus' daughter Pithane it is likely that she died and was buried before the chest was commissioned. Her bones were subsequently exhumed and reinterred in the family chest.

A third chest, larger and more fancifully decorated, was found in the cemetery lining the road to Magnesia which was apparently reserved for Roman and native dignitaries and officials. The inscription was repeated and enlarged on the stone pier supporting the chest:

> To the departed spirits of Titus Valerius Secundus, son of Titus, a soldier in the 7th Praetorian Cohort in the century of Severus [on the chest]. Titus Valerius Secundus, son of Titus, a soldier in the 7th Praetorian Cohort in the century of Severus. His home was in Liguria. He served eight years in the army. He served in the garrison at Ephesus. He lived 26 years 6 months [on the pier].

The cremated bones of one individual were found inside the chest. The shape of the hip joint indicates a male. His age (about twenty-six) may be inferred from the state of the sutures on the cranium, which are at the point of fusion, and from his teeth (45).

In this instance, where more detailed information is given in the inscription, there is a remarkable coincidence between the evidence of the text and that of the bones. The soldier of north Italian origin apparently died without family or heirs while on active service. His tomb at Ephesus was respected and left undisturbed. Fragments of glass were found fused to the ends of his long bones (46), showing that glass vessels had been thrown onto the funeral pyre. In all five cremations the pyres appear to have been lit below the centre of the body, which was still fleshed when burnt. The extremities were less burned and the fingers and toes fell to the base of the pyre in the course of cremation.

45. Cremated remains indicative of age and sex. From the cinerary chest of Titus Valerius Secundus, who died at Ephesus. Sc.1275.

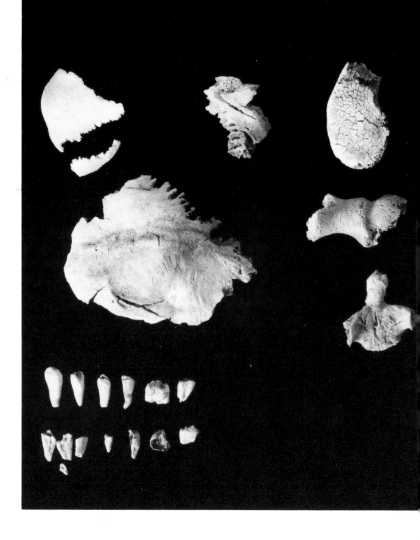

46. Fragments of glass fused to the long bones of Titus Valerius Secundus.

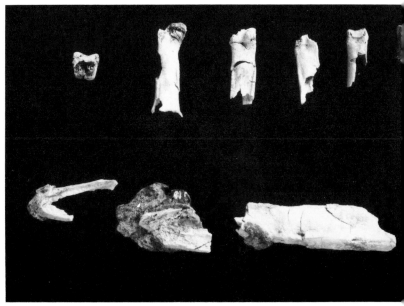

After burning the remains of the pyre were raked out and the bones were collected together to be broken into fragments before being packed in the chests. Part of a pig's femur was found in the chest of Titus Valerius Secundus, possibly an animal that was sacrificed at his funeral.

No evidence for burning of animals was noted from other burials. In other respects, as far as we can tell from the surviving evidence, the cremation rites of the Greek inhabitants and of Roman officials resident at Ephesus appear similar. And though the chests were of a type peculiar to Ephesus, their form did not greatly differ from that of some chests made in Italy (GR 1958.4–17.1,2). References in the surviving literature of the later first century AD affirm that cremation might take place at the site of burial or in a special area reserved for the purpose: the careful collection of the bones, which were raked free of ash, suggests that the latter may have been arranged for cremations at Ephesus. It is said that the corpse's eyes were opened before placement on the pyre, and that (as at Ephesus) personal effects and even pet animals might be burned at the same time: compare the instructions given in the will of the provincial notable Sextus Julius Aquila (p.16) and the gestures made at Augustus' funeral by soldiers who had served him with distinction (p.7).

Gifts for the dead

While out riding in the summer of 1860, Frederick Crowe, British Vice-Consul at Benghazi (Libya), noticed that his horse's hooves gave out a hollow sound when moving over a certain rock. Further investigation revealed a tomb of a type commonly found in the eastern Mediterranean. An oblong chamber cut in the rock was flanked on both long sides by recesses designed to hold sarcophagi. Several of these, made of lead or marble, were discovered. Two marble sarcophagi evidently intended for children (23) were sent to the British Museum along with some of the finds from the tomb.

Crowe's drawings have unfortunately perished, but some account of the discovery of the tomb and its contents is preserved in his letters to Charles Newton, then Keeper of Greek and Roman Antiquities at the British Museum. In the circumstances it is possible to locate the find-spots of only a few objects. The children's sarcophagi were found in the same recess. Beside them were found several fragments of painted plaster figures representing two youths as *erotes*, and an ornate pottery lamp. Less certain is the context of a pottery *pyxis* (cosmetic box), said to have been found in a sarcophagus, the identity of which was not specified, two terracotta figures, a terracotta head 'found at the entrance to the tomb', part of a carved bone box, a green-glazed jug and two marble portrait busts carved in relief.

In the skull of one of the children buried in the marble sarcophagi was found a coin, apparently of late fourth- or early third-century BC date. This may have been placed in the child's mouth to pay the ferryman Charon. The terracottas and the *pyxis* are of similar date to the coin. The other objects found in the tomb are Roman, but none (with the possible exception of the plaster figures) is contemporary with the marble sarcophagi, probably made during the reign of the Emperor Hadrian (AD 117–38).

An interesting sidelight on trade is offered by the contents of this tomb: the Greek objects were made locally, but the Roman objects were mostly imported from Italy, Greece and Asia Minor. Some were domestic objects of high quality; others had a religious significance. The plaster figures may have been intended to suggest that the children buried in the marble sarcophagi were in death to be regarded as *erotes*; a figure of Eros adorns the centre of one of the sarcophagi. The most likely explanation of the range of objects is that the tomb, designed for multiple burials, remained in use for about five hundred years.

The very fragmentary objects found with cremated bones in the cinerary chests from Ephesus are of much more limited range, representing glass and coarse pottery vessels of local manufacture, made at about the same time as the chests (AD 50–120).

The status of tombs

The cremated bones found in Anassa's chest (p. 55) indicate that two people were buried inside it, though only one individual is named in the inscription. The second burial may have been sanctioned by the family of Anassa, since there is evidence to suggest that both bodies were cremated at the same time. The inscription set up on the tomb of Aurelia Felicissima (p. 18) includes a stern warning to those who used the tomb without the right to do so. Such admonitions were very common, especially in Asia Minor, where the violation of tombs seems to have been a recurrent problem. Another text from Halicarnassus cursed the violator: 'May the land not be fruitful for him nor the sea navigable. May he have no profit from his children nor a hold on life but may he encounter utter destruction' (*GIBM* 918).

Under Roman law tombs were the property of the *Dii Manes* (the spirits of the departed), to whom funerary texts were customarily dedicated. The container of human remains, whether sarcophagus, urn or chest, was regarded as sacred and inviolate. The aura of sanctity might be extended to the tomb or chamber in which the burial casket was set. According to the jurist Ulpian, writing in the third century AD, 'the statues decorating a tomb, even those not sealed or fixed, are not private property. They form a body with the monument in the same way as cinerary chests, urns and sarcophagi, and all belong to the *Manes*.' But emperors, often subject to fits of moral indignation on being offered evidence of gross personal wealth amongst their subjects, regarded gardens, sculptures and other memorials around the tomb as extraneous frivolities not subject to the laws on the sanctity of tombs. This is clear from the responses of Trajan, Hadrian and, in the third century, Philip, to petitions on the subject.

Funerary art and symbolism

It is hardly possible at a distance of two thousand years to recapture in detail the symbolic meaning of the decoration of Roman funerary monuments. Opinion on the subject in recent times, much of it marked by Christian views of the individual experience of the afterlife, has verged from the enthusiastic interpretation of every cupid and festoon, to the sceptical view that many were unaware of the details of their order from the marble workshop. Certainly the drastic alterations made to unsuitable sarcophagi and reliefs bought from stock speak of an interest rooted in earthly rather than spiritual matters. But options were no doubt narrowed by the available choice, and by the frequency of premature death, which entailed hasty purchases. Some of the themes depicted on Roman sarcophagi seem quite inappropriate, even tasteless: 'How would you like to have a man who killed his mother, a woman buried alive, or a child's collapsed chariot as a pretty ornament for *your* tomb?', wrote one despairing modern historian of Roman funerary art.

The selection of a decorative theme drawn from Greek tragedy may have had moral purpose: intellectuals such as the writer Lucian and the Emperor Marcus Aurelius (AD 161–180) wrote that tragedy had the power to instruct audiences in morality, and was devised to recall the events of life. Many contemporary sarcophagi were decorated with scenes taken from the stories of Jason, Medea, Alcestis, the Leucippidae and Laodamia, moving tales of love, death and the triumph of *virtus* (manly courage and probity). Often the arrangement of the scenes recalled events on stage; some of the features in the background resembled parts of Roman stage buildings.

Towards the end of the second century tragic subjects began to fall from fashion, to be replaced by tales of the deeds of Hercules, Paris and Mars. Bacchic subjects, suggestive of a paradisiacal existence, retained their popularity throughout the second and third centuries. As the market for sarcophagi expanded to a greater range of social classes, demand grew for themes drawn from life, and individuals began to take the place of the hero or heroine of a myth. Portraits set in shells or medallions supported by cupids or figures of victory may have reflected an increased tendency to represent the dead as heroes.

Mythological figures on sarcophagi made in Greece and Asia Minor were largely drawn from repertoires of traditional interest to the areas in which the sarcophagi were produced. Rome was the centre of interest in myth and drama, and in the representation of individuals as heroes. It is perhaps worth recalling the wider-ranging influence of Greek dramatic themes upon early imperial wall-painting, and, more significantly, upon Etruscan funerary art. A similar fascination with Greek drama had been displayed by those who purchased painted vases in the semi-hellenised areas of southern Italy. Many such vases were destined to be grave-goods. Some of the dramatic themes of south Italian vase-painting are so obscure that their meaning is now lost to us. No doubt in imperial Rome, as in, say, Lucania, in the fourth century BC, the display of erudite knowledge of the classics conveyed an impression of civilisation and refinement.

It is hardly surprising, so strong was the association between the use of sarcophagi and the widespread adoption of other aspects of Greek culture in the Roman world, that the 'climate of opinion' about the afterlife (a term coined by the historian of religion A. D. Nock in the absence of evidence for organised belief) favoured the *mousikos*

47. A man declaims his works, attended by a muse. From a Phrygian marble sarcophagus found at Rome. Sc.2312.

48. Part of the sarcophagus of Marcus Sempronius Nicocrates. Sc.2313.

aner, the man of Greek culture. He is personified by Proclus (p. 16) and by the figure illustrated here (47) declaiming his works to a muse set in the adjacent niche of a Phrygian sarcophagus. The cultured man was not above self-mockery, as is shown by the sarcophagus of Marcus Sempronius Nicocrates (48), with a Greek epigram proclaiming that his former respectable identity as 'a man of Greek culture, a member of a troupe performing at festivals', was exchanged for the less tiring life of a pimp. 'But even in death', he proudly concluded. 'the muses take charge of my body'.

Memorials and the stranger

No less than extravagantly decorated urns and sarcophagi, the texts of Roman funerary monuments were intended to attract the attention of strangers, not bound to the dead through obligations of kinship or dependance. Our sympathy may be directly enlisted: 'Traveller, stop and read, for nothing could be found crueller than this monument' (p. 44). The text may invoke a sense of awe. An inscribed portrait herm, a figure with the torso in the form of a shaft (originally used to mark a boundary), invites the reader to 'Recognise Rhoummas when you look at him in a portrait carved in marble, a man who performed great [deeds of] faith through prayer; dying, he did not indeed die, for he came by a good repute' (49).

The injunction 'Recognise' is perhaps to be taken literally, for the man portrayed above the text is evidently blind in one eye. The attempt at realism is all the more remarkable for the memorial having been cut from a statue; the buttocks of the original figure are visible at the base of the rear of the shaft, and folds of drapery dent the crown of the head. A large notch, evidently belonging to an earlier period of use, is cut in the right side of the shaft. The figure from which this was cut may have resembled statues of the god Hermes. The name Rhoummas is well attested in the region of Syria. Here white marble would have had to be imported from distant quarries, which may explain careful reuse. The style of the portrait is reminiscent of the revival of the traditional Roman style in the late first century AD; the style of the lettering suggests a date no later than AD 150.

The last phrase of this text clearly expresses the desire of the pagan

49. Memorial herm to Rhoummas. From the Levant. GR 1948.10–19.1.

dead for eternal memory amongst the living; immortality may be gained through *fama* (a good reputation) built up in life. Greek and Roman funerary inscriptions were designed to be read aloud; in so doing, we are to speak for the dead: 'Be aware, traveller, that your voice is really mine' (*CIL* XIV 356, a marble tablet found at Ostia). Some were worried that the reader might be too bored to care: 'I pray you read it willingly, and read it again, don't let it bore you, my friend' (*CIL* XI 627, the tombstone of Aulus Granius Stabilio, freedman auctioneer, of Ravenna). Boredom might be averted with wit: 'I've died many times'. confided the manager of a troupe of actors from Siscia, now in Yugoslavia, 'but never like this' (*CIL* III 3980). There was nothing like a joke at the reader's expense. A relief carved on a slab closing a *loculus* (a small vault which held a coffin) portrays a skeleton (50). Above is carved the mocking inscription: 'Who can tell, passer-by, having looked at a fleshless corpse, whether it was Hylas [the epitome of youthful beauty] or Thersites [the epitome of ugly senility]?'

The individual was as much evoked in words as in a portrait in stone. Emotionally demonstrative at funerals, the Romans had no place for the dead at the centre of their religious belief. The dead lived in the carefully cultivated memories of others: drawing on a symbolic language used for centuries by various peoples of the Mediterranean, the stones of memory offered a long-term prospect of immortality.

50. *Loculus* decorated with a skeleton and a text mocking the reader. From Rome. Sc.2391.

Further reading

B.F. COOK, *The Townley Marbles* (London 1985)

F. CUMONT, *After Life in Roman Paganism* (reprinted New York 1959)

H. HÄUSLE, *Das Denkmal als Garant des Nachruhms* (Munich 1980)

K. HOPKINS and M. LETTS, 'Death in Rome' in K. Hopkins, *Death and Renewal* (Cambridge 1983)

G. KOCH and H. SICHTERMANN, *Römische Sarkophage* (Munich 1982)

J.A. NORTH, 'These he cannot take', *Journal of Roman Studies* 73 (1983) 169–74

R. REECE (ed.), *Burial in the Roman World* (Council for British Archaeology Research Report 22: London 1977)

J.M.C. TOYNBEE, *Death and Burial in the Roman World* (London 1971)

R. TURCAN, 'Les sarcophages romains et le problème du symbolisme funéraire', *Aufstieg und Niedergang der römischen Welt* 16, 2 (Berlin 1978) 1700–35

Where to see the sculptures in the British Museum

An asterisk indicates an illustration in the text.